Identity

JOSEPH DENNIS

authorHOUSE®

AuthorHouse™ UK
1663 Liberty Drive
Bloomington, IN 47403 USA
www.authorhouse.co.uk
Phone: UK TFN: 0800 0148641 (Toll Free inside the UK)
*   UK Local: 02036 956322 (+44 20 3695 6322 from outside the UK)*

Published by AuthorHouse 10/28/2020

ISBN: 978-1-6655-8158-5 (sc)
ISBN: 978-1-6655-8157-8 (e)

About the Book

Who are you?

Like this is a genuine question that every person with a pulse has pondered at some point in their life. And within these short words of poetic artistry I hope to get you thinking. Some words and emotions are significantly so real to many they may lead you to cry or vent. I wrote these words bearing in mind that our stories are not over. If you have breath in your lungs, a pulse; then you must keep going. My heart behind this is for every soul that picks this up and flicks through the pages, to reflect and remember that you have a greater purpose on earth that just where you are.

Your thoughts and words have power.

The Journey Alphabet

A is for all the arguments.

B is for the bass of the music.

C is for all the conflicts within each heart.

D is for all the disasters in education.

E is for all the envy.

F is for all the failures.

G is for all the grades we achieve.

H is for the happiness we strive for.

I is for the information we need.

J is for the jokes we enjoy.

K is for the constant kicking of toddlers.

L is for the laughter we love.

M is for the minute silence.

N is for negative influences.

O is for the opportunities to correct ourselves.

P is for the people who have helped us learn.

Q is for the quietness.

R is for the responsibilities one has to endure.

S is for the seasonal greetings.

T is for the teachings.

U is for the unity of a nation.

V is for the visions we aspire to achieve.

W is for the world we live in.

X is for the kisses in love letters.

Y is for the yawning we naturally have.

Z is for the snores we hate.

Imagine

Imagine a world of peace.

Imagine a life without hatred.

Imagine witnessing the birth of a child.

Imagine the abolition of bullying.

Imagine a day of joy and happiness.

Imagine the amazing discoveries we've yet to find.

Imagine a world of no knowledge, peace, hope, or accomplishment.

Imagine high school once in a while.

Imagine the worldwide traditions and becoming one.

Imagine yourself ten years from this very moment.

Imagine your lifelong achievements.

Imagine your life as a blessing to others.

Imagine!

You Say, I Say

(Your mind is an enemy.)

You say 'conflict', I say. 'peace'.

You say, 'stress', I say, 'blessed'.

You say, 'discouragement', I say, 'encouragement'.

You say, 'broke', I say, 'wealth'.

You say, 'loss', I say, 'gain'.

You say, 'no', I say, 'yes'.

You say, 'cloudy', I say, 'sunny'.

You say, 'thoughtless', I say, 'thoughtful'.

You say, 'hard', I say, 'easy'.

You say, 'panic,' I say, 'peace'.

You say, 'useless,' I say, 'useful'.

You say, 'sadness', I say, 'happiness'.

You say, 'challenging', I say, 'simple'.

You say, 'exam', I say, 'test'.

You say, 'weak', I say, 'strong'.

You say, 'conflict', I say, 'serenity'.

You say, 'lifeless', I say, 'lively'.

You say, 'old', I say, 'young'.

You say, 'hopeless', I say, 'hopeful'.

You say these things that only make me stronger.

My mind!

Change

(One perspective through the eyes of a 16-year-old boy.)

The true unity of the world, is it so obvious that everyone has emotions?

Is it so obvious and clear that everyone has a voice? Is it so obvious and precise to count the never-ending deaths as they consume all people: old, young, man, woman, boy, girl, human?

Why do the words we speak affect us so bitterly, emotionally, physically? Why do we allow the actions of the voiceless to dictate our futures? Why does society have so many divisions despite the world being a place of harmony?

Think about the losses of great people. You lived through that challenge; they didn't.

'Terrorism, terrorist,' they say. Do you really know the true story of calling someone a hurtful word? Their backgrounds? Their childhoods?

We can relax and watch the world deteriorate. We can really emphasise the need for migration, jobs, and the economy. We can do all of these things, but how does this change society?

The actions. The words, the sound, the mind, the connection.

The embrace of unity has become forgotten, all that remains are …

Fear! Deceit! Crime! Bullying! Negative actions with no proper intentions or reasons.

Calling someone worthless.

Why?

Because they're different? Because they live in a broken home? Because they're black? Because they're from an Asian background?

How do all these thoughts, actions and mindsets set that prime example of increase, success, unity.

Through the eyes of a 16-year-old teenager who sees the unity of the world becoming a reality. Through the feet of a boy who thanks and shows signs of gratitude daily.

Not many can understand how positivity shields the negative influences around him.

Only society has changed the way his thoughts operate. Society is a gift. Gifts leave marks on someone. Someone you may never see again.

Again! Again! Again! Again into a-gain. Gaining what you're taught, educated-lifestyles. Crime lurks around every vulnerable spot in your life.

Society is going through challenging period. Societies change. People change. Change brings people closer. Yes, it's hard to believe, but change has many perspectives!

Now!

It's up to you to be that change. A 16-year-old student. A poet. A teenager.

A human who has seen the struggling, challenging societies and has opted for the new step into restoration.

Society has changed! I have changed! Time changes! Nonetheless, be yourself for you don't know the future of our society. Society and the future.

Society is you.

Change!

The Power of Anxiety

The true reason for this life, isn't it written in the stars?
Well, maybe things don't all end in the sky.
To be honest, I don't know why I'm here.
It's like everyone is telling me one thing,
While my mind tells me something else.

There is this one thing that sees to target the 'weak'.
There is this one thing that is destroying the minds of children.
There is this one thing that never stops; it just doesn't stop!
Stop it!
Just stop!
I might as well die and forget I even existed.
The funny thing is, nobody cares.
It's like my mind is working with the devil.

If you're wondering what I'm on about,
It's,
It's,
It's,
It is the emotion that forgets you are even human!
Like, why attack me? Why? I've done nothing wrong!

'Life is what you make it.'
Them quotes aren't gonna help me.
Like really, words don't mean anything to me if this emotion is still
hurting the ones I love.

OK, I've had enough!
I'm taking this knife and rope.

Y'all don't need a compass to find me.
I'll tell you where I'll be.
Down there,
Down there,
Down in that cemetery.
Yep,
I'm gonna end it all,
Just gonna finish what the devil wanted me to do.
I'm gonna commit suicide.
It's not like anybody really cares for me.
All this nonsense about hope; how is there hope when I'm suffering?
You know what?
I'm done.

Heartbeats—
The never-ending beating of a heart.
Isn't life worth living?
Well if this emotion has turned from an issue into a burden, then do something to nullify the pain.
Pain only gets worse if hidden.
To hide emotion is to hide the true extent of your situation.

Take this analogy of a clock.
There are twenty-four hours a day, correct?
More than twenty-four people hold back this emotion.
If time was to reverse, would this emotion even exist in that person's life?

I place my heart on my emotions.

If this poem makes your experience with this emotion negative, then stop reading.
I'm not here to expose your flaw.

For anxiety is not a flaw; it's an emotion with a weakness.

The weakness is up to you to discover.
You have to make the choice.

For me, I'm overcoming anxiety daily. How?

My faith in Christ.

I'm alive because of him.
I'm just like you.
I'm just like you.
I'm your brother.

You see, anxiety is just ... I apologise; anxiety is not 'just an emotion', it's a disease.
It rots away your joy.
It destroys your liberty.
It will remain an 'it'.
It doesn't deserve a name.

Guess what? Anxiety will go.
It will leave your mind.
The scars you have, you don't have to be ashamed of them.
They're there for a reason.

Anxiety, guess what? You have no room in my life.

You're really annoying; heck, so many things in life are annoying.

Guess what? I survived committing suicide.

I'm an example,

A strong example of overcoming anxiety.

Those who have fallen short of overcoming this powerful emotion are soldiers who deserve a medal.

A medal that says, 'A soldier not overcome by anxiety but overcame many challenges.'

I sign off.

I sign my signature into a life filled with joy, peace, and Christlike desires.

I sign my mind into the mind of Jesus.

I say anxiety is powerful; however, it's not the *most* powerful challenge in our lives.

Life is a blessing.

Emotions are blessings.

Love is a blessing.

And I choose the most powerful emotion—

Love.

Miracles

The miracle of life. The miracle of life. The miracle of life.

It'll take much more than three phrases to express the miracles that we fail to realise.

For myself, miracles can change, develop, or maintain things.

The miracle of life.

The miracle of life.

It's no random cause that we're alive.

You may have felt low, those constant negative thoughts.

Miracles don't appear for a random reason.

Miracles have that positive sense of compassion.

The miracle of life.

The miracle of life.

'Don't take things for granted':

I'm sure you've heard that phrase before.

If not, then I must tell you that everything can go within the heartbeat of a child.

The miracle of life.

The miracle of life.

I walk.

I can speak.

I can run, laugh, and fall down and get back up.

I can express my emotions-despite the world being the barrier for those negative influences.

I can see, taste, smell—the five senses are part of my life;-thank you!

I have wonderfully annoying siblings, but I love them.

I have a caring mother, a soldier of an uncle-who's trying his best to discipline me; despite all the mistakes I make, he keeps me going.

I can talk to my friends.

I can smile.

I can write poetry.

I can do all these things because they're miracles from God.

The miracle of life.

The miracle of life.

Together we share this miracle.

Together we block those negative thoughts.

Together miracles allow us to do so many things.

The miracle of life.

The miracle of life. The miracle of life. The miracle of life.

I hope you've realised why these phrases are significant to me.

Miracles happen every day.

I hope to be a miracle to as many people as I can.

That inspiration.

That poet.

That miracle.

Life.

The One Who Had My Heart

Every day,
Lord, let me be yours.
Please, God,
I'm so sorry for all the pain I've done to everyone.
Lamenting about myself isn't healthy;
Thanking you for life is.
Rejecting the lies of the enemy,
The lies of the world.
My heart is just so warm for you,
Compassionate Jesus.
Hallelujah!
I found you.
Sixteen-year-old me
Found grace
On that wonderful cross.
Your blood,
Your body,
Your shouts of pain don't compare to mine.
The joy of the Lord is my strength.
Let be and be still, and know that I am God.
You're my Shepherd.
May you guide me continually in your love and
Grace.
Thank you.

Conversations with God

I am a wondering soul on Planet Earth,
Fighting the consequence of sin,
Trying to gain worth in societal and cultural
Commodities.
That doesn't change the fact that we're all equal—
Money, greed, relationships, despair,
A Jesus-believing, God-fearing young man
Plagued by the sins of self.
Sins caused by rebellion,
Guilt caused by feeling inadequate
And indulging oneself in 'good vibes',
Only to realise that good vibes don't change
Who you are.
They allow you to dwell in the sacred realm of peace,
Not perfect though.
The only perfect peace I know—and this is within
My soul—
Is that Jesus died for me.
Not only for me
But for you.
Religion condemns you.
Jesus transforms you,
A relationship that lasts all eternity.
Yet lost souls still don't believe.
This soul must do all he can to fight this sinful
Nature of humanity
And press onwards.
What's a little rain without the muddy plains?
I am the one to change young people.

I am one of many who believe in the Gospels of Jesus.
And in this journey,
I want to love more,
Love harder,
Love deeper,
Care more,
Speak far less than increase the mess.
Listen to the cries of the world,
And have the faith to trust in you.

Pull That Trigger

Dear thoughts,
remember me?
When was the last time I let you in to distort my
reality,
the realness of death?
Oh, yes,
it's not blessed.
Death is a curse.
My mind sometimes goes crazy
when I hear the sound of that trigger.
I see it's bigger.
I lie face down on my bed sometimes,
wondering how in the world I'm still alive.
Aisle 9, death is here.
Come purchase your automatic nooses,
£1 per shot.
Down this vodka, and stay right up.
Can't you see it's more than me?
I blink and thank God that wasn't the last.
Maybe I should just blast myself.

Then I take another breath.
That's not my story.

Dig

Think for a moment that your life is a book.

Each year from your birthday until now,

All the crowds,

Crying out loud.

You remember a particular time in your life.

I can't remember if there was strife,

But you know everything was all right.

You're travelling to school,

To work,

To a business meeting

In the acceptance,

On the bus,

In a car,

And your mind is travelling at immense speed.

Just for this memory,

You traverse childhood,

Teenage-hood,

Adulthood.

And eureka,

You found the memory!

It holds a lot of precious moments.

Your mind is roaming;

Your emotions are connected.

To what, you may ask?

Well, you, your memory.

You were once scared of something.

And bam, an image pops up.

Look up and see the sky.

That changed too.

You have the power to rule,
Not in earthly kingdoms.
But if you're a son,
Remember to run
Towards your identity.

I Will Not Be Silenced!

A wooden cross
It was made to destroy,
It was made for death.
But it was all a decoy for the real power of God
To be revealed.
Marvel at the finished work of Jesus!
He said those words 'it is finished.'
He's won,
And because he won,
We are partakers of that victory.
How could I not see
That the Romans meant to silence him?
Oh, dear souls,
You can't silence someone whose entire life was
Dedicated to serving others,
That man we call Jesus.
He did just that,
The ultimate sacrifice,
The ultimate form of humility beyond
Imagination.
He was not silenced.
He stood his ground.
And yet we sinned
And keep on sinning.
He died.
Let that sink in.
He actually died.
Here's the evidence of true meekness:
He chose to do it.

He was not silenced.
Nor are we.
So as we look to that tree,
Not on a piece of jewellery,
I decree that
I will not be silenced
For the harvest is plentiful,
And the labourers are few.
So I'll live my life in remembrance of you,
Jesus,
I love you.
You weren't silenced
So that I could have the voice to declare your
Love.
Your finished work lives on.

I'll Take That

2,000,
2,000,
2,000.
It's an interesting number, isn't it?
2,000.
2,000 pounds,
2,000 dollars,
2,000 people,
2,000 miles per hour,
2,000 years.
Now that's something different.
I'm not here to isolate this number based on
Opportunities we get in life.
For all we know, we strive throughout our entire
Lives.
It's so bright ... until it's not satisfying our earthly
Needs:
Sex,
Immediate gratification.
For every nation has fallen.
We fell from this word called "grace".
It's a tough race,
Like a tennis player smashing that ace.
U
It's a steady pace.
A wooden tree
Where he died for me,
Oh, it's so wonderful to see
That he actually died for you.

It's hard to believe, right?

His body dangling on that cross,

Symbolising severe loss.

But oh so beautiful it was

Because it was so broken

And yet so whole.

He died for you.

Can't you see it too?

You see all the pain in this world?

Sin is the cause of it all:

Governments,

Nations,

Killings,

Suffering.

We fail to take ownership for the things we've done

To one another

When God sent his only Son:

'Forgive them for they know not what they do.'

Remember he died for you.

He was more than a martyr.

He was and is the ultimate masterpiece,

And he wants you to come home.

Now before you read the next line, let me tell you

Something about my journey,

How he turned a little old soul

From a lying human

To a wholesome soul.

The need of grace.

Unmerited,

Unearned,

Undeserved

Favour
From God.
We can't earn something he freely gave;
It's a gift.
A death that shocked the entirety of human
Existence
Still impacts lives today.
So what will you say
When your days are done
And there's nowhere to run?
Will you be satisfied with the life you lived,
With the people you hurt,
With the jobs you had,
With the career that earned you,
With the family you raised
When your soul was longing for a relationship
with your Maker?
Come home, dear soul.
This moment is what he died for:
'Forgive me, Father, for I'm a sinner, I need you, all
Of you. I'm sorry for how I've been. I need you. I
Need you. Your love is more than enough for me.
Take me home, hug me, embrace me. I love you,
Jesus. You're the Son of God. I'm ready to follow
You on this journey called life. Amen.'

Welcome home.

So Will I

It's interesting how my heart works. How you
created my mind and my body. Grace like none
other. The animals bow before you. I should do
the same. I gain something. It's called love. A
better understanding of who you are. The birds
praise you. The waters rush by rhythmically. And
people call me crazy because I'm more sensitive
than other guys. That's me. I choose to write.
Writing opens my soul to your goodness. 'And as
you speak.' As I live, let my soul embrace you. I'm
fearful love of you. All you. And not me. Take me
out of the equation, God. Just let me be the vessel to love others. I don't
care who they are,
what they've done. I care about grace. Hope.
Laughter. I want to be that believer who loves
unconditionally. So will I worship the earth? Or
you? That's the question that doesn't need to be
pondered. For it is written, 'Seek first his
kingdom ad his righteousness, all these things
will be given to you as well.' If the animals can
praise and live for you, so will I.

We were made to be a poem.

You were made on purpose for a reason in this
Season.

It's not Even Stevens.

You know who you're becoming

Under the sun,

Where there's nowhere to run.

Sorry, I Messed Up ... Again

Tick-tock,
Tick-tock,
Tick-tock,
I ran down the block.
God, why am I so prone so anxiety,
To mistakes,
To failure,
To being frozen midsentence,
When I try to speak up,
About things I care about,
People I care about,
Your cross, Jesus,
Just peace,
Hope?

...

Forget I even started a conversation with you
Because this human is tired of messing up.
Jesus, grant me the grace to keep going,
Keep going,
Step by step,
Day by day,

...

My mind loves to dwell on negativity
Or the past mistakes I made.
Even a conversation not too long ago
With a loved one sparked guilt,
Privacy,

And peace.
Lord God, lead me through this valley
Full of setbacks
And turns,
And lead me in your will for my life.
Stop being distracted, Joseph,
For your victory is right there.
Just look forward.

Perspective Change

I'm not ashamed of who I am because if I was,
it would be an insult to God, who made me.

Value

Some people don't understand who Jesus is and what he's capable of doing.
Rather, they prefer the religious perception of a man who died on a cross two thousand years Ago.
Guys, he's real and alive
If you're willing to accept his love.
This evening I've never cried so much whilst reading God's Word.
Not even a whole chapter
But two verses
Confirming who God says I am:
Anxiety,
Stammering,
Body looks,
Glasses,
My nose,
Social anxiety,
Suicide.
Those things became a target for the devil to manipulate
Over and over and over and over again!
I've been in so much pain over my identity in Christ,
Plagued by despair and depression.
For so long I've held back speaking life into myself.
I encourage others,
But pain has stopped me from helping myself.
God's Word is all I needed tonight.
The fear of feeling/being worthless,
I'm 100 per cent not the only person in this position.
Whatever you find value in,
Is it going to carry you through life?

Or are you gonna compromise your identity to feel accepted?

That has been me

In relationships.

Not being able to do simple tasks,

Not being able to listen or learn as quickly as others—

It's painful,

Painful to the point where suicide every now and again

Tries to break into my soul.

Yet

I'm fighting,

Not by my strength,

But by the cross of Jesus,

Who took all the worthless comments, gestures, lies that people and the devil have used against me and you.

Enough with the hate.

Love each other.

Words have power.

Deteriorating inside,

Mental health is important.

People only care if they are going through it.

Care now.

Be compassionate.

And boys and men in particular,

It takes more of a man to be compassionate and loving

Than to be muscular

And 'hard' (whatever that means).

Just keep going, soldiers.

Like me.

Me

If I had a dollar for the number of times people said I looked ugly
because of my nose,
If I had a dollar for the number of times I've had to pick myself up
Because of insecurities,
If I had a dollar for the number of times I've held back from saying
negative, hurtful things to someone,
If I had a dollar for the number of times I've thought about ending it all
Yet I'm still here,
If I had a dollar for the number of times I've wanted to hug people and
backed out
Because I was scared of what people might say,

I'd be very rich
But broken.
I'd rather be this way because I am me.
I'd rather be this awkward guy,
I'd rather be this person who likes to inspire,
I'd rather be this flawed human,
I'd rather be positive than hurtful,
I'd rather be tired because I've helped someone live a little longer
Than be tired because I've battled anxiety so much.
And you, reading this caption,
If you would rather be someone else,
Then that's a waste.
Fight those insecurities.
Be proud of who you are.
I love my hair.
I love my body.
I love my skin colour.

He made me this way,
Compassionate Joseph,
Any Joseph,
Annoyed Joseph,
Passionate Joseph.
I can take pain, oh yes.
But there's only so much one person can take.
I'm still here,
And so are you.
Let's be this light.
C'mon, you wonderful soul,
Don't give up
For you are priceless.

You're priceless.
You're loved.
You're definitely worth it.
You're amazing.
You're beautiful.
You're awesome.
You're flawless.
You're wonderfully made.
You're not an embarrassment.
You're crafted to do positive things.

If 2017 wasn't good year for you, forget it; life
Doesn't waste time in giving us an easy ride.
You gotta push
And never give up.
You, beautiful soul, are precious.

Never forget that.

For a Reason

What if our paths never crossed
along this journey called life?
Every soul you meet
is here for a reason.
We can change to be kind,
to show love,
or we can forget that a human being is behind
the phone.
Grant positivity, and never let it go.
You reading this,
did you know you're priceless?
Yeah, this world says some strange things.
Forget the world.
Focus on you,
the real you,
be genuine,
be authentic; let the real you shine.
No one likes a copycat,
so stop trying to be like others.
Why try to fit in when you were born to stand out.

My Heart Beating

You must keep going
while this world is throwing,
throwing hatred,
sorrow, and pain towards each other.
The thing is,
we say words we never physically see,
yet we're surprised when someone remembers
what you said to them further along time.
Cherish your loved ones.
Yes, I'm human too.
Yes, I'm flawed.
But don't tell me I don't have a voice,
one that gratefully proclaims the faithfulness of
Jesus Christ.
I am one of many souls yearning for more of him.
You know so many young people die daily
because of the words spoken to them,
words used as weapons.
I really wonder what those people's heart
condition is.
For sure they've been through something.
You reading this should not judge those who've
hurt you.
They're human, too,
like that boy you shouted at,
like that sibling you ignored last year.
And like that friend from church you forgot to text

whose about to … to … to

pull that trigger.

Life is so precious, dear soul.

Let's live like it.

Your heart just took another beat.

Cultrary

Here goes:

This world is messed up.

It doesn't take long to see that

When you could be a prat and ignore.

How could you ignore what the poor are going

Through?

Just as a ripple starts by the pool,

Here's the new rule: 'love your neighbour as

Yourself.'

But truly,

It's unruly,

News breeding the lies of morality.

Somehow people think they're on the side of

Immortality.

Here's the reality:

Children get hurt,

Hurt people hurt people,

Everyone needs somebody,

The church is breaking from the inside out.

But I believe in the revival of the gospel.

Spell the word backwards, and you get the state

Of humanity.

Forget Jesus,

Forget God,

Forget faith,

Forget the lies of the enemy.

No, not humans,

The enemy.

You wear the devil horns

While others are deep-rooted in anxiety.

You forgot how precious you are.

The hour is soon to come

When everyone will bow to the King of Kings.

It'll ring in your head,

The cries of this world.

Are you really proud that you hurt her?

He just overcame suicide,

And you say, 'Man up!'

What the hell is that?

We forget that we're broken too.

Human,

More like offended.

This offended generation is as toxic as the pain of mental illness.

You must keep going.

These words are just a shadow

Of the grace that Jesus showed on that cross.

Culture is _____.

Be careful of who you're surrounded by.

Check your heart.

You're a masterpiece.

Inside Outside

These thoughts you know.
It's more than what you sow,
It's what you reap as well.
Whether it's internal
Or external.
Keeping them inside my mind
Is like poison.
That's why I slowly find the remedy in sharing,
Sharing my story.
Healing is within the words we speak.

Mosaic

Mosaic.

I am me.

I am me.

I am me.

No one can say otherwise.

I am me.

Someone created me.

This being knows me.

He knows my life is challenging.

He made it like that.

I am me, and now I see who I'm meant to be.

A mystery, that is what life is.

A challenge, that is what life is.

Choices, that is what life offers.

A choice that my mind fights every day.

That is suicide.

It's not an easy word.

Nothing in life is easy.

My life is full of squares,

A confusing puzzle creating who I am.

I am me.

One square is my body.

This teenage body is weak.

This human body is weak,

Always demanding something.

Water.

Food.

Energy.
Something science has developed called
Medicine.
Not science but human beings created that.
I am me.

Squares, squares, squares.
My life is made out of squares.
One square is my personality.
Creativity.
Sensitivity.
Laughter.
Sadness.
Encouragement.
I am me.

A large part of my life consists of many squares.
This is my faith.
Jesus.
That man who died on that cross for me.
I am me because of him.
Church.
Choir.
Prayer.
Struggles.
I am me.

My flaws, now that's what make me unique.
Unique in every way.
Striving for a breakthrough each day.
Remembering to pray.
That's good until reality causes you to feel

Ashamed.

Oh, boy, am I flawed.

My flaws make me who I am today.

Squares, my flaws complete lots of squares.

My … mental … squares,

Determined to sway me left and right.

Determined to force me to quit.

I gotta say I've contemplated suicide a lot.

Never giving up.

I'm a soldier.

They interfere with my confidence,

The biggest square anxiety.

What nonsense it makes me do.

Not talking to anyone.

Allowing negativity.

Suicidal thoughts.

C'mon, you're better than that, Joseph.

You're better than suicide, all of you young

People.

These squares contaminate my life.

There's this one square I've saved for last.

I call it my special square.

It has my family.

Friends.

Loved ones.

My creativity.

My poetry.

My memories.

My future.

One which God has granted me.

I am me.
Regardless of anxiety.
The truth is
I'm trying my best.
I cry on my heart countless times.
I'm positive because I'm preventing anxiety and
Those negative squares from harming what's
Important to me.
I am me.

I am a mosaic of one life.
A life of chances.
A life of mistakes.
I am me.
A mosaic.

Printed in Great Britain
by Amazon